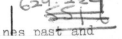

TRACTION ENGINES
PAST AND PRESENT

Burrell showmans road locomotive *Earl Haig*, 7nhp three-speed compound No 3979 built in 1924 as a road locomotive and converted for showman E. Symonds, Gloucester in 1934. Restored from an incomplete derelict by the present owner.

TRACTION ENGINES PAST AND PRESENT

ANTHONY BEAUMONT

DAVID & CHARLES : NEWTON ABBOT

BY THE SAME AUTHOR

Traction Engine Pictures (3rd imp)
Traction Engines on Parade (2nd imp)
Rally Traction Engines (2nd imp)
Traction Engine Prints
The Organs and Engines of Thursford (2nd imp)
Steam Up! Engine and Wagon Pictures (2nd imp)
Fair Organs (2nd imp)
Traction Engines and Steam Vehicles in Pictures (2nd imp)
A Gallery of Old Timers
Ransomes Steam Engines—An Illustrated History
Fairground Steam

0 7153 6379 4

© **Anthony Beaumont** 1974

Set in Plantin
and printed in Great Britain
by W J Holman Limited Dawlish
for David & Charles (Holdings) Limited
South Devon House Newton Abbot Devon

Contents

ABBREVIATIONS

SC   single cylinder

SCC   single-crank compound cylinders

PE   ploughing engine

nhp   nominal horsepower. The term originates from the Royal Agricultural Society of England who tried to equate the power of early steam engines with the work done by horses. In more accurate terms, the actual brake horsepower output was approximately five times the nhp for continuous working and up to eight times for very brief periods.

The Working Years

The density, weight and speed of commercial road traffic today, the internal combustion mechanisation of agriculture with harvesting in one operation, makes the age of steam a comparative fantasy. Yet throughout the Victorian era and into the twentieth century, the United Kingdom's great industrial and trading expansion depended entirely on steam as a mechanical heavy mover.

If the sun then never set on our empire, that sun was always shining somewhere on our steam machinery at work, helped by live horsepower and manual labour.

Together with the basic mechanical simplicity of steam traction, portable and the smaller stationary engines, their great virtue was the ability to keep going when atrociously neglected or damaged. This was common overseas where unskilled natives tended engines miles from a railhead or good road.

In Assam, a portable worked for years with steam jetting from boiler rivets damaged in an overturn. The workmen merely dodged the leaks and stoked up to combat them. A large duplex cylinder mill engine worked on one cylinder, its partner being badly cracked.

At home, traction engine haulage, slow and sometimes hazardous, coped with loads in excess of 100 tons. Drivers and mates lived and worked hard. They dealt with breakdowns and sometimes were killed en route by winding cables, runaways and occasionally by boiler explosions. The steam men's lot was slightly less arduous only in the late 1920s and early 1930s. The final steam wagons outclassed gear-grinding petrol lorries and steam drivers in their enclosed cabs were quick to gesticulate about this supremacy when overtaking.

In farm and field steam thrashing tackles and pairs of massive ploughing engines alone in a vast landscape grappled with the incessant toil on the land. In the 1880s a steam plough driver's wage was about 18s weekly for some sixty hours including overtime, while the 'cook boy'—perhaps fourteen years old—received about 6s.

Thrashing was a back-breaking aggravatingly dusty job, but while the engine's exhaust beat rose and fell all the long day, the labour had to endure. Winter timber-hauling needed two tractions in wet conditions. If one became bogged, the other cable-hauled it out. The tree trunks were also loaded and the 'drag' winched bodily through the mud by the engines' winding cables.

Despite all these difficulties, the men gaze from the earlier photographs in this book with a serenity indicative of a way of life which could be forecast from father to son. Their skills were inherited and learned in the same way.

Eighty years ago, £2,500 outlay for a set of double engine ploughing tackle and £600 for a traction, were considerable sums even for large landowners. Apart from a few accidents caused by negligence, steam men were well able to carry their employers' trust.

The pictures of steam at work in rural scenes and peaceful roads now long-forgotten or obliterated by 'development', tell a more interesting story than one continued in words.

(*above*) Allchin three-shaft traction built c1880 shown with thrashing tackle outside the *Fox & Hounds* in the Peterborough area. Date uncertain but probably about 1905. (*below*) Sussex thrashing in the 1920s with Allchin No 901 8nhp traction built in 1896 and the first four-shaft design from this maker.

(*above*) Allchin 7nhp compound traction No 1427 made in 1905, seen here at Gravely, Herts in May 1945 when owned by T. T. Boughton & Sons Ltd. (*below*) Working Aveling & Porter rollers owned by G. T. Cushing near Fakenham, Norfolk in 1960. The nearest engine is No 11322, single cylinder, built in 1926.

Aveling & Porter traction built between 1874 and 1884 shown in the 1890s with Army Royal Engineers at a South Coast resort generating for 'flood lighting' the hotel. A 'lash up' light appears extreme right.

Aveling & Porter single cylinder three-shaft, single-speed traction built in the early 1870s, thrashing in Hants about 1880. The copy photograph shows a cast royal arms plate similar to F. Savage's design (dating from 1875) on the drum end.

Aveling & Porter 4nhp compound tractor No 6021 built 1906. Shown about 1910 with water pipes load for Rickmansworth and Uxbridge Valley Water Co at Batchworth, Herts.

Aveling & Porter single cylinder traction No 2333 built in 1888 hauling a thrashing drum in September 1936 when owned by Bishop of Aston Clinton, Bucks.

(*above*) Aveling & Porter 4nhp compound tractor setting off from J. G. Peele, Wymond-ham, Norfolk, with a Christmas turkey load for London in 1913. (*below*) Burrell single cylinder traction No 931 made in 1883 thrashing in September 1935 in the ownership of H. E. Challand, Rippingale, near Bourne, Lincs. The canopy is the original fitting.

Burrell SCC traction No 2003 *Diamond Queen* new in May 1897 to R. Old & Co, Charlton Marshall, Dorset. Photographed about 1904 when owned by W. Cooksley & Son, Long Sutton, Somerset, the owners until 1953. Rebuilt in 1962 and preserved.

Burrell compound tractor 4nhp, two-speed, spring mounted, seen here in 1921 when hauling the complete village hall for Hingham, Norfolk.

Burrell SCC traction, probably No 2496 built in 1902, blowing off vigorously when owned by W. Foxley, Manor Farm, Bookham, Surrey. A fine character study of enginemen and labourers.

Foden compound road locomotive No 417 6nhp built in the early 1890s and seen here in October 1944 when owned by T. Forth & Son, Staxton, Yorks. The rear axle springs can be seen above the rear wheel.

Fowell (St Ives, Hunts) single cylinder traction No 96 7nhp built in 1906 with thrashing drum in September 1935 in the ownership of C. Portass, Long Sutton, Lincs.

(*above*) Foster three-shaft traction No 2373 8nhp made in 1899 working at Moulton Chapel, Lincs in 1935 when owned by F. Thorpe. The engine still exists. (*below*) Fowler single cylinder ploughing engine No 2051 12nhp built in 1873 shown with a full head of steam between pulls at Latimer, Bucks about 1910 in ownership of T. T. Boughton & Sons Ltd. The high gear pinion is on the footboard.

Fowler single cylinder PE 14nhp built in the early 1870s at work for Ward & Dale, Sleaford, Lincs a few years before the beginning of World War I. The friction band on the rear wheel is the differential and the brass casing to the Salter safety valves well fits the tea-kettle!

Fowler two-speed traction built in the mid 1870s with thrashing sets at Alton, Hants, probably in the early 1880s when owned by Wrights of Alton.

A pair of single cylinder Fowler PEs (rebuilt by John Allen & Co as set No 5) with cultivators, water cart and crew of six.

(*above*) Fowler PE No 3448 built in 1877 or '78 with detachable change speed crank-shaft pinion and rebuilt with a Burrell SCC cylinder block. Shown here with culti-vator. (*below*) Fowler class B6 road locomotives *Talisman* No 16263 and *Vulcan* No 14844, when owned by Norman Box of Manchester, Birmingham and Leeds, hauling 137 tons net load in the late 1920s.

Fowler compound PE class BB1 *The Little Helpmate* No 15176 16nhp built in 1918, pulling hard for J. Gray, Hadleigh, Suffolk in July 1950.

A fine composition of Norfolk thrashing in full swing. Definite information unknown but the locality may be Kerdiston in the mid 1920s. The engine appears to be a compound Fowler built in the 1890s.

Fowler compound hauling and winding traction No 14963 7nhp built in 1918 for intended Russian export. Photographed in 1938 near Rudham, Norfolk with thrashing set. Owned by O. Rix, Sculthorpe, Norfolk.

Fowler compound PE No 13997, built c1914, one of the pair of largest PEs used in the UK and supplied to Lincs; cylinders 9in and 15in x 15in. Seen here at APCM Cherryhinton Cement Works, Cambridge in September 1935. The pair were exported to Malaya in 1950.

(*above and below*) A cross section of the villagers of Tivetshall St Mary, Norwich in 1901 on the occasion of the felling of a giant oak. The main trunk shown was 19ft long, with a 21ft girth, and weighed 20 tons. The engine seen is a single cylinder Fowler PE built c1885.

Fowler PEs class BB1 No 15219 (foreground) and No 15218 built 1918 with cultivator tackle and full steam pressure, preparing to work at Witney, Oxon in 1952. Owners were Griffen and Melhuish, Bruen Lodge, Oxon.

The last traction—No T17—built by C. J. R. Fyson of Soham, Cambs in 1924. The boilers were bought out and Burrells supplied the cylinders. The special taper bolts securing spokes and rims can be seen here when setting to the thrashing drum.

Garrett 5 ton compound 4nhp tractor on springs with enclosed two-speed gears, owned by the North Eastern Railway. Shown hauling a 7 ton capacity Garrett trailer probably in Poppleton Road, York in 1915.

(*above*) Hornsby traction No 6317 6nhp built in 1882, set up for thrashing at Thurlby, Lincs in September 1935 when owned by D. Stanton, Boston, Lincs. (*below*) Special steam shooting brake for Wood, Sudbourne Park, Suffolk, built by Lancashire Steam Motor Co (later Leyland) about 1902. The vehicle has a twin vertical engine and a final belt drive.

Londonderry undertype 5 ton capacity steam wagon No 41, built at Seaham Harbour Works, Co Durham. Seen here in 1915 in ownership of the NER outside Easingwold private railway station, Yorks. The platform details include an NER poster for 'Motor Char-a-banc Tours'.

Londonderry undertype steam wagon No 38 with Ackerman steering on a centrally pivoted and sprung axle. Photographed about 1915 at Station Rise, York in front of NER No 1 Fire House—since demolished and replaced by NER War Memorial.

Mann & Charlesworth (Leeds) light traction No 54 7nhp, built c1900 with single eccentric reverse gear. Shown in ownership of John Croft, Naburn, Yorks in September 1944. In 1908 the successors of Mann & Charlesworth were Mann's Patent Steam Cart and Wagon Co.

(*left*) Marshall Colonial
duplex cylinder portable
with spark arrestor and
large firebox for wood fuel.
Photographed when new
c1910 at Marshall's
Britannia Works, Gains-
borough, Lincs. (*below*)
Marshall single cylinder
traction No 24156 6nhp built
1894 or '95, thrashing
when owned by J. Thackray
& Sons, Brawby, Yorks,
in September 1944.

Thrashing near Horsmonden, Kent in the early 1930s with a compound Marshall traction, owned by C. Lambert who is seen on the extreme left against the engine's tender.

37

Marshall single cylinder traction No 23644 8nhp made in 1894 with thrashing tackle on original wheels. Shown here in October 1944 at Brandsby Bank, Yorks when owned by J. Word, Grimstone, Yorks.

(*above*) St Pancras Iron Works, London, 5 ton capacity undertype steam wagon built between 1907 and 1910 and photographed in use by the NER in 1915 or earlier. (*below*) Robey traction built in the early 1880s and having outside steering chains to a narrow tracked front axle. Shown set to a thrasher when owned by Gibbons of Castor, Northants.

Ransomes Sims & Jefferies 7nhp compound road locomotive on springs, photographed when new about 1910 at Orwell Works, Ipswich. The restrained lining out applied to ordinary tractions will be noted.

RS & J compound three-speed road locomotive 8nhp No 24967, built in 1912 for the Rt Hon The Earl of Pembroke, Wilton Estate, Wilts. Photographed at Ransome's main entrance 1912.

RS & J compound traction No 37087 6nhp built in 1926 shown here in September 1946 with two thrashing drums and elevator in the ownership of F. B. Gibbons & Sons, Market Deeping, Lincs. The engine exists.

(*above*) Savage steam wagon, with F. W. Savage centre, at King's Lynn Great Eastern Railway station in 1907. The bronze statue of King Edward VII for the Grammar School new buildings has just been loaded by hand crane. (*below*) Chain drive Savage traction built c1875 and fitted with hand-turned low gear meshing with teeth inside the flywheel rim; thrashing for Lord Northesk at Binfield, Berks about 1882.

(*left*)
Wallis & Steevens
compound 4nhp
'oil-bath' tractor,
probably built in
1903 but certainly
the first mechanical
vehicle to be used
by the Post Office
in 1905. Seen here
in 1910 or soon
afterwards.

(*below*) Tasker
Little Giant com-
pound tractor
No 1741 5nhp
three-speed, chain
drive made in 1917,
shown timber haul-
ing at Amersham
Common, Bucks
for F. H. Grover
in April 1933. This
engine went to
Tasker's museum,
Andover and exists
in private owner-
ship.

Wallis & Steevens 8nhp traction built in the early 1880s, photographed when nearly new in the railway yard at Basingstoke, Hants.

The second design of Wallis & Steevens 3 ton single cylinder tractor loading timber deep in a Surrey wood near Guilford in the early 1900s.

One of the first Wallis & Steevens 3 ton single cylinder tractors No 2418 made in 1898 photographed when new with a brewer's demonstration load.

(*above*) Wallis & Steevens $4\frac{1}{4}$ ton tractor with a good load when owned by Spencer & Co, St Mary Cray, Kent. Probable date of photograph 1910-12. (*below*) Road tar patching near Lewes, Sussex in 1910 with a Wallis & Steevens 3 ton tractor built in 1905. A tar barrel is on the winch for hand-loading and pouring.

(*above*) Wallis & Steevens 5 ton 4nhp compound 'oil bath' tractor built c1908 with a W & S two-way plough on the recreation ground, Seaford, Sussex in 1916 during the war-time food drive. (*below*) Thrashing near Lewes, Sussex in 1920 with an 8nhp W & S traction fitted with flywheel brake when owned by A. French, Seaford.

Wallis & Steevens single cylinder traction No 7226 7nhp built in 1911, thrashing at Gt Missenden, Bucks in September 1936 when owned by C. Evans & Co.

The Preservation Years

The two friends racing their traction engines at Appleford, Berkshire in 1950 aroused general preservation interests besides amusement in that unique spectacle.

The preceding fifteen years had been very good ones for scrap dealers cutting up steam vehicles. It was therefore a fortunate chance which caused many owners to pause for reflection before parting with their remaining obsolete engines for about £1 per ton. In any case a very few machines would have been preserved for nostalgic reasons or business acumen.

The 1939-45 war years resurrected steam for vital work. Fowler ploughing engines were the only available means of winching PLUTO (pipe lines under the ocean) fuel lines on the Channel beaches. Showmans and road locomotives worked at demolition during the London 'blitz'. Generally, a disused but not derelict traction or showmans cost between £30 and £60 in the late 1940s and could be put in good order for a modest sum.

The first organised gathering of traction engines was also at Appleford in 1953 and soon other rallies were attracting a thousand or so spectators. National, and a growing number of regional steam clubs eased restoration problems and maintained interests during the winter. The upsurge in car ownership contributed very much to successful rallies.

Although 'cheap' engines were becoming scarce, repairs were still helped by the numbers of scrapyard tractions awaiting either destruction or a buyer. One inexperienced purchaser was dismayed when a boiler inspector's hammer went straight through the firebox of the recent 'treasure'.

By the 1960s, rising costs were making difficulties in running an engine 'on a shoestring'. A rally condition traction was then worth about £800 and a showmans up to £2,000, the former being the approximate new price. There were still a few derelict engines languishing in remote places, quietly rusting solid and disintegrating beyond recall. The desire to own a brass-enriched showmans locomotive led to a number of traction engine conversions—sometimes to the dismay of purists.

Wisely, the earlier engine racing had now been replaced by demonstrations of authentic work, thereby encouraging a preservation sideline in thrashers, balers and large sawbenches.

Ploughing engine owners have their own society and ploughing demonstrations have probably opened more eyes to the sheer power of a steam mechanism than has anything else on the rally field.

Nowadays a large proportion of engines are owned by business concerns of some mechanical aspect and situated in our remaining rural areas. Owning a traction engine is hardly a practicable idea in mushrooming, tightly packed communities, apart from the initial cost which has doubled during the past ten years.

A steam engine is not a casual plaything. Its potential dangers are recognised by the National Traction Engine Club among other organisations and of course, by knowledgeable owners and drivers. The most important document for a steam engine is its boiler test certificate.

The low-loaded, immaculately finished engines, profusely lined out (and even chromed here and there) are indeed a far cry from the working years. But the regular chonk of the exhaust, the gearwheels ringing, a clutchless lunging start of ten tons of metal and the grime of coal and oil all remain unchanged.

Aveling & Porter compound PE No 8890 *Marshal Haig* built in 1918 and photographed in 1967 between plough pulls when the fire had been made up (see *Traction Engines & Steam Vehicles in Pictures*).

Some of the less glamorous work of engine ownership: an Aveling & Porter light road locomotive No 9149 5nhp compound built in 1928 under renovation at Thursford, Norfolk in 1962 and showing some interesting constructional details.

(*above*) Aveling & Porter single cylinder 8 ton 6nhp roller No 10121 built in 1921 and formerly owned by Perth & Kinross CC (Scotland). Seen here in 1972. (*below*) Aveling & Porter compound 4nhp tractor No 11486 made in 1926. Conspicuous features are this firm's all-cast wheels and narrow and deep boiler water tank.

(*right*) Probably the oldest Burrell traction to survive and dated about 1878. The 8nhp single cylinder carries a pair of Salter safety valves and the weighted governor is a mid nineteenth-century design. Shown here at Weeting, Suffolk in 1972.

(*below*) Burrell No 1244 built in 1886 8nhp traction which remains with the Desborough family business at Magdalen, Norfolk since new as their first engine.

Thrashing at Pakenham Mill near Sudbury, Suffolk in 1960 with the only existing SCC Burrell portable, No 2363 built in 1909. This engine is now in the Bressingham collection.

(*right*) Burrell SCC traction No 2528 built in 1901 showing its original cast-iron chimney. The 'Patent Engine' on the smokebox door refers to Burrell's arrangement of the compound cylinders. (*below*) Burrell single cylinder traction No 2963, two-speed built in 1908. In common with all existing Burrells, this is a three-shaft design, shown at Woodton in 1961.

(*left*) Burrell SCC traction
No 3307 7nhp two-speed
built in 1911 and seen here
in 1959. The diagonally
arranged compound cylin-
ders and change speed gear
pinions are clearly seen.
(*below*) Burrell showmans
locomotive *Western Pioneer*
No 3871 7nhp compound
new to S. Stokes, Ipswich
in 1921 then with Cole's
Amusements, shown when
fitting new smokebox
in 1962.

Burrell single cylinder No 3607 built in 1914 at work in ownership of C. Aldrich, Norfolk in the early 1960s. The vertical handwheel operates a band brake working on the second shaft.

A compact Burrell compound road locomotive No 3777 5nhp three-speed built in 1918 and used in a Somerset stone quarry. Photographed in 1971. The normally copper pines are iron because of wartime economies.

(*right to left*) Burrell compound crane engine No 3829 6nhp built in 1920. Allchin single cylinder traction No 669 7nhp made in 1890 and Burrell SCC No 2386 7nhp built in 1901. Seen here at Horsham, Sussex in 1967.

Burrell compound traction No 3686 7nhp built in 1915 with a thrashing load at Docking, Norfolk in October 1971. Apart from the baler's pneumatic tyres and some belt guards the picture could well be in the heyday of steam.

Burrell showmans locomotive No 3878 *Island Chief* 6nhp compound built in 1922 and formerly owned by Robert Payne, Hull, then Arnold Bros, Isle of Wight. Photographed in 1961 generating for an eighty-nine key Marenghi organ.

Clayton & Shuttleworth single cylinder traction No 43187 7nhp built in 1910 thrashing in Norfolk in 1960. In 1968 this engine was owned in Yorkshire.

(*right*) A single cylinder Clayton & Shuttleworth traction after partial renovation showing well the details of boiler construction and cylinder mounting which are normally hidden by the wood lagging and its covering metal sheets.
(*below*) C & S single cylinder traction No 47015 built in 1915, seen here at Hannington, Northants in 1962.

Foden showmans locomotive No 2104 *Prospector* 8nhp compound made in 1910 and one of the two remaining Foden showmans. Shown here in the ownership of W. Hicks, Little Stanbridge, Essex at Battersea Park, London 1972.

(*right*) Foden 'Sun' overtype tractor No 13730 built in 1931 and one of three of the type fitted with pneumatic tyres. Duplex cylinder enclosed poppet valve engine and water-tube boiler. (*below*) Zettlemeyer (Germany) compound piston valve roller No 553 built in 1930. The 6nhp cylinder block is unlike any English design. Shown in London 1972.

Foster compound traction No 14564 5nhp built in 1926. The inclined valve spindles are visible above the trunk crosshead guides.

R. BAXTER & SONS, EYE, PETERBOROUGH.

Foster single cylinder traction No 14622 8nhp built in 1930 photographed at Chatteris, Cambs in 1963.

(*left*) Fowler single cylinder tractor 5nhp No 18640 built in 1913 with enclosed steering gears and a very good set of rubber tyres, shown at Stamford in 1967. (*below*) Fowler's last and finest showmans locomotive No 20223 10nhp compound built in 1934 as *Supreme*. Restored over many years from dereliction to original perfection including chromed decorations.

Fowler showmans compound tractor No 14798 3½nhp made in 1919. The working order weight is approximately 5 tons compared with an average 18 tons for 8nhp showmans engines. Photographed in London 1972.

(*above*) Fowler PE class AA No 13877 *Sir John* 18nhp built in 1916 entering Ransomes' Works, Nacton, Ipswich in July 1971 where the Ransomes'-made John Fowler's first steam-hauled plough was tested in 1856. Steering, K. Steward, owner of the two. Driver, F. T. Dyer of RS & J who drove their last traction from the works in 1934. (*below*) Fowler PE BB1 No 15421 *Sir John's Lady* also entering Ransomes' Works.

Fowler single cylinder PE class KK new in 1914 shown in 1959 after cutting up en route to Woodton Rally because of a broken rear axle. The owner is in the centre.

Fowler PE class BB1 No 15334 16nhp built in 1916 shown in working order and appearance in 1960. The standard dust covers over the slide bars are in place.

Sixty tons of Fowler class BB1 PEs at Hannington, Northants in 1962. (*left to right*) Nos 15363 (1919), 15218 and 15219 (both 1918). All owned by J. Bennie, Holcot, Northants.

A pair of Fowler PEs class BB1 No 15336 (*foreground*) and No 15337 built in 1919. Photographed at Elseworth, Cambs in 1956.

Preservation at Lake Goldsmith, Australia in 1969. Fowler class R compound traction 7nhp No 9836 built in 1903 and exported to Melbourne Agents. The tender rails are for wood fuel.

(*left*) Garrett compound tractor No 33380 4nhp made in 1918. Shown here travelling at 12–15 mph at Chatteris, Cambs in 1963. (*below*) Another Garrett tractor No 33278 built in 1918. This was the firm's best-selling type and made from 1907 to 1928.

Garrett compound tractor 4nhp No 32944 made in 1916. Photographed in 1961 when recently 'rally finished'.

McLaren compound tractor No 72808 4nhp *May Queen* and a rare example today. Seen here in 1972 at Weeting, Suffolk.

One of the last showmans locomotives to work on the fairground and used until 1957, McLaren No 1623 10nhp compound *Goliath* built for the War Department in 1917 as a road locomotive and said to weigh 25 tons as a showmans engine.

(*left*) Marshall traction No 37690 single cylinder 7nhp made in 1902. This is *Old Timer* owned by and shown here with Arthur Napper at Appleford, Berks where they raced in 1950. (*below*) Marshall traction No 69269 two-speed made in 1914. Seen here at Stamford in 1964.

Major H. D. Marshall's Marshall traction No 45415 7nhp new at the Gainsborough Show in 1906. Photographed with the owner at Marshall Sons & Co Works, Gainsborough, Lincs in 1964.

The traction engine at home in rural peace—Marshall No 69254 7nhp new in 1928 (*right*) Marshall single cylinder traction No 85554 7nhp built in 1925 photographed at Raynham Hall, Norfolk in 1963. (*below*) Marshall traction No 87005, a single cylinder four-shaft 8nhp and one of the last designs built in 1934.

Marshall twins in 1960. (*left*) No 83780 7nhp, (*right*) No 83600, both built in 1928

Marshall portable single cylinder piston valve No 82196 made in 1926. The wheel construction is peculiar to Marshall portables. Shown here in immaculate finish at Weeting, Suffolk in 1972.

(*left*) Ransomes Sims & Jefferies traction two-speed No 33156 built in 1922, seen here at Dunmore Park, Ulster, N. Ireland in 1970. (*below*) Robey 4nhp compound tractor No 37657 built in 1918. The two-speed gears are completely covered and a rear wheel brake is fitted.

Robey portable with duplex cylinders No 40062 made in 1920 and in process of renovation. There are twin protected water gauges and a boiler-mounted safety valve.

Arriving at Revesby, Lincs rally in 1963. (*left to right*) Ruston & Hornsby traction 6nhp No 161250 made in 1930, Ruston & Hornsby portable 4nhp built in 1921, Walker (of Tewkesbury) centre engine, duplex cylinder built in 1887.

Sentinel DG6 waggon No 8213, twin cylinder undermounted engine, built in 1931. Normally the rear axle is chain-driven from the leading bogie axle which itself is seen chain-driven from the second shaft of the enclosed engine unit.

Super Sentinel undertype tractor, chain-drive No 6504 made in 1926. The lower part of the vertical boiler and Ackermann steering details are detailed.

(*above*) Sentinel waggon S6 shaft-drive under-type built in the early 1930s—the firm's final UK design. These 'clean exhaust' steamers were 'forced off the road' by axle loading restrictions and cheap diesel fuel. (*below*) Tasker tractor No 1296 built in 1903, named *The Horses' Friend* and given by two ladies to the RSPCA for assisting horse transport up the Crystal Palace hills, S. London.

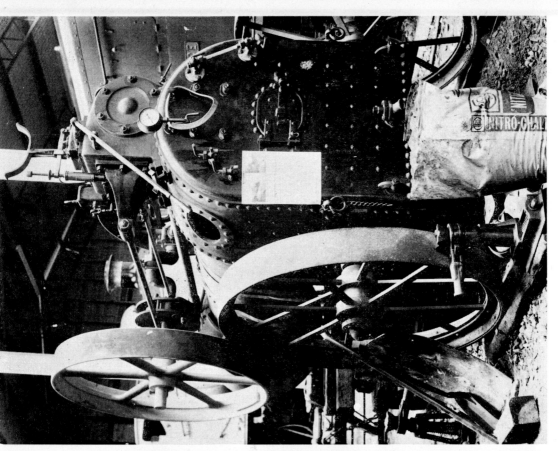

The only existing example of a portable made by E. Youngs, Diss, Norfolk, a single cylinder 8nhp with the very rare feature of a crankshaft Hartnell centrifugal governor coupled to the valve rod. (Bressingham Museum 1969.)

Yorkshire wagon 4nhp 3 ton capacity No 940 built in 1917 with the firm's unusual centrally fired horizontal boiler placed across the wagon front.

Acknowledgements

John P. Mullet for extensive use of his historical collection; *Eastern Daily Press*; *Lynn News and Advertiser*; Brighton *Evening Argus*; *The N. Yorkshire Moors Railway Preservation Society*; *The World's Fair*; *Steaming*; Ransomes Sims and Jefferies Ltd, The Post Office, W. C. Baker, Miss B. Copinger-Hill, F. T. Dyer, B. French, A. Hall, C. F. Lambert, R. Mallett, Major H. D. Marshall, B. Phillips, Mrs Joyce Rushen, C. Smyth, E. Snelling, R. H. Temple.

The majority of the pictures in the preservation section are from the author's camera.

Index to Plates